Advance Praise

"In John Sibley Williams' "amalgam of real /and fabled light"
one is able to believe again in the lyric poem as beautiful—if
difficult—proof of private space. As with families, histories, selves,
Sibley writes: "we like to believe / what we make will save us."
Disinheritance contends intimately with loss, to be sure – but it also
proposes the poem as a way to remember, to persist, to be oneself,
to believe. And to persist when belief may not be possible within the
bounds of the shores the seas impose upon us."

—Joan Naviyuk Kane

"There is eternal longing in these poems of John Sibley Williams.
A yearning for what cannot be understood. A song for what simply
is. A distance beyond human measurement. The dead and alive
dancing, hurting, and praying at the mouth of what must be the
beginning of time. A series of profound losses giving birth to words
no different from medicine."

—Zubair Ahmed

"There is a hunger in these poems, one of an empty handed wise
man who wants to sing. And sing he does. Here in *an amalgam
of real / and fabled light,* stones ask questions of rivers, as the
poet *reaches toward the temporary holiness of knowing.* These are
mostly his words because how else can one speak of what the poem
offers, but through the poem. Let these poems sing to you too. Let
them hold you in that *raw place of hope,* let them be *ships mooring us
to the wild / bottomless sea.*"

—Daniela Elza

"In John Sibley Williams' moving, somber collection, the power of elegy, reverie, and threnody transcends the disinheritance caused by separation. These compellingly atemporal poems form the locus wherein generations of a family can gather. Here, Williams' lyric proto-language—elemental, archetypal, primordial—subsumes barriers of time and space. His poems create their own inheritance."

—Paulann Petersen, Oregon Poet Laureate Emerita

Disinheritance

John Sibley Williams

Disinheritance

John Sibley Willams

Apprentice House
Loyola University Maryland
Baltimore, Maryland

First Edition

Printed in the United States of America

Paperback ISBN: 978-1-62720-131-5
E-book ISBN: 978-1-62720-132-2

Design: Itzayana Osorio
Editorial Development: Alexandra Maule

Published by Apprentice House

Apprentice House
Loyola University Maryland
4501 N. Charles Street
Baltimore, MD 21210
410.617.5265 • 410.617.2198 (fax)
www.ApprenticeHouse.com

info@ApprenticeHouse.com

For my mother, always

The author extends his heartfelt gratitude to the following journals and anthologies for previously publishing poems, some in different versions, in *Disinheritance:*

Analekta Anthology (Boho Books) – In Apology, Salmon Run, and
     Calligraphy
The Blue Hour Magazine – Ceremony, Fertility, and Miscarriage
Bodega – A Dead Boy Fashions the Grand Canyon from His Body
Booth – In the Kingdom of Moths
Brittle Star – A Dead Boy During the Dry Season and A Dead Boy
     Distinguishes Proximal from
Distal
Bryant Literary Review – Sanctuary
Chiron Review – November Country
Cirque – I Sit My Grandfather by the Mouth of the Columbia River
Cricket Online Review – A Room for Listening
Event Magazine – Away from Stillness and Penance
Freshwater – Say *Bang*
Grey Sparrow Journal – The Cultural Narrative of Clouds and To
     Name Butterfly
Handsome – Forth and Back
Lake Effect – Alight
Life and Legends – Frontiers
Literati Quarterly – Eulogy
Lunch Ticket – Denouement
Nebo – A Dead Boy Fishes with His Dead Grandfather, A Dead Boy
     Learns Metaphor, and A
Dead Boy Speaks to His Parents
Osiris – Truce, House on Fire, A Dead Boy Visits the Grotto, and A
     Dead Boy Counts
pacificREVIEW – Grief is a Primitive Art
Penumbra – Mother's Day and Lullaby for the Damned

Prelude – Echo Chamber

PRISM International – A Dead Boy Martyrs His Mother

Radar – Teething and Things Start at Their Names

Red Paint Hill – Hemophilia

The Scrambler – Paean and Preparations Have Been Made

Sequestrum – Oppenheimer, Pompeii, and Optimism

Skidrow Penthouse – Procession and Postpartum

SLAB – This Place of Scraps

Third Coast – Bone River (all parts)

Willow Review – I Go to the Ruined Place

Xanadu – For My Mother, in Parting

"Hemophilia" was a finalist for the *Hawai'i Review*'s Ian MacMillan Award.

"Bone River" was a finalist for the *Third Coast* Poetry Prize.

"Grief is a Primitive Art" won 2nd place in Oregon Poetry Association's 2015 Contest.

"Denouement" was an honorable mention in Oregon Poetry Association's 2015 Contest.

Contents

III.

Look: no one ever promised for sure
that we would sing. We have decided
to moan. In a strange dance that
we don't understand till we do it, we
have to carry on.

William Stafford
from "An Introduction to Some Poems"

I.

Bone River (i)

Our child experiments with her
limbs, displacing air and
waiting for the vacancy to fill.
Such a raw gesture—
raw and enigmatic remorse.
What is it here I have done
and am waiting for?

       For what it's worth, love,
a stone asks the same
question of the river.

Have I broken you yet?

Truce

A panic of finches rises and tonight
the late salmon moon is filled

with rivers and old shadows. Reflected,
iridescing, an amalgam of real

and fabled light. I rub grains of wood and cloud
between my hands and stretch from the grass

into a grandmotherly story of angels,
their necessary demons, and how little

it takes for the one to climb or descend into
the other. This is what she told me before

she climbed or descended. The distance from us was
the same. This is how she explained where I'd gone

and am going.

My hands don't remember much anymore
of where the birds have flown. There are felled trees

in the sky. The moon's face drifts across the river.

And I miss the hard geometries of coffins.

Salmon Run

The river comes bloody to our shore and we are thinking
less of causes than how to abstain from drinking.
Hands form a perfect cup, our mouths oval into

a perfect thirst. It is hard

but a good thing to say *no* sometimes
to these choiring fish and violent incisions of sawgrass.
It is good, this struggle. The heavens
and the earth can only keep us

inside so long. Shores erode and all
of a sudden we are chin-deep and vanishing
upstream in bundled schools toward whatever it was our
great-grandfathers were,

toward the temporary holiness of knowing
all my mistakes have been made before.

    River, angry

old river, I understand your need to run
swiftly from the source. I too don't look back
at the mountains, so distant, dawn-red,

where I am headed to spawn.

November Country

My grandfather digs a double plot
with his bare hands in case winter
can be shared
though he knows grandmother will outlive
her heart's thaw by a decade.
I could give him a shovel. Instead

I ball the half-frozen river's slack
numb around my fist, tighten
into ice. I will try to be less
hard next time.
Here in the gray
and two-dimensional house
we know the answer to rain.

A perforated black
arrow of birds moves
southward, away. Shrill reports
from every side and from the sky
the trajectory of abandonment.

Our surfaces are like the river.
Our circles have learned
to grow edges and crack.
Even the birds
we compare ourselves to

have left us.

Syncopation

Once we believed the animal
heart, ceremonially extracted from flesh

and swallowed, free of our own
distortions, would drive us,

healed,
toward eternity.

*

How we got here, together,
is clear enough.

A white doe tracked across
whitest winter.

Indents in earth deep
as the body can manage

and behind them our own
unerasable prints to follow home.

I eat the landscape with the whole
of my eyes. White doe, whitest field,

shared, empty, the nourishment I expect
from taking in her heart.

However much I eat,
there is not enough *forever*

woven into her body
to heal me.

      *

Language breaks down
like this: *you*

must in some way suggest the *I.*
The world must break

inward. My heart
must be there, in yours,

or nothing.
I have nothing but this need.

Yours is the doe's heart I must eat
to remember why I'm here.

Grief is a Primitive Art

No one taught me
how to draw this bedroom—

in undefined charcoal,
with the immediacy of crayon,
erasable pencil,
permanent ink,
stone upon stone
upon wall?

Should the light source
be celestial
or inherent to our hands?
Either way
it seems angled
away from your face.

For background, to include
our broken reflections
or an empty mirror?
And how long
can the flowers
I brought you
retain their color?
Can you even see them?

Arbitrarily I've decided

to depict the sheets
as a cancer,
your body a shadow,
our tears an empty vase,

and faith
has forever been rendered
a shallow cup
inches from our lips.

Ceremony

Though it is deep
unreturnable winter,
I am told to open
all the windows
in this room of too many
exits.

Snowflakes beat themselves senseless
against your moon-blanched face
and in melting smother
the ritual candles
we've left burning all day,
all night, and will reuse
soon enough.

Something like prayer
but without the certainty
flutters aimlessly between us
with no place to land.

Our breath is the air
and the air is opaque.

There is a fever-pitched giving
and an inevitable taking.

Forbidden, the cold light
we're left with
hurts the stars
and the stars aren't
in your hair
anymore.

Father writes "open"
on your forehead in ash
while I trace "tomorrow"
on the white sheet
of your eyes
going still.

A Dead Boy Speaks to His Parents

Hush now;

you don't have to be   anymore.

Whatever script you'd written for the stars to follow, they've missed
their marks,
gone true right   instead of stage right.

Nightly, you whisper:
ever since   *perhaps because*   or *even before* —

but you don't have to thread cause through effect

or rummage through whatever beginnings you've captured on film to
discover a fixed point of departure.

The zoetrope continues to spin   without image.

Mom and Dad;

you don't have to be   contained anymore

between the lines I never had time to write
on the stars   that don't listen anyway.

Things Start at Their Names

Ice locks the river in place and my heart
is static for the season and traversable.

Sometimes a boy about the age
my son would be adventures

half way across me before remembering
the duty to destroy the one thing

beneath him. He writes his name
on my rib; it says *Curiosity*. I reply

with the name I've learned to wear:
Distance. A fluster of bluegill follows his body

downstream to where it meets the Columbia,
in time the ocean, which I cannot make freeze.

Next spring I will snare the things that still move in me,
beat them against stone, and eat until empty. I have

his name written all over my body; it says *Forever
be Winter*. My wife calls him *Gabriel*; after all these years

she still calls him *Gabriel*, and sometimes from the shore
she calls to me: *Thaw*.

Paean

There are trees here
hungry for nutrients you'll soon bequeath them.
There are microscopic creatures
who know coffins endure the elements only so long.
And I hunger alongside them,
wondering if voice ends
with its body.

Yes, the shovel has already
forgotten your name,
the stone has forgotten, and the wood,
perhaps one day the photographs and house.
But the earth is patient
as a sapling's first leaf,
indifferent yet ravenous.

Someday if I am devoured
by the same gnawing roots, perhaps
your tree will remember me.

Oppenheimer

Mother we call the nourishing earth, the unbroken
cradle, the raw and refined works
outside us. Whatever water follows the river
without belonging to it can be traced
to that primitive art of holding another
over your heart, then releasing. *Son*

and *daughter* and *lover* and *home*, how purified
we emerge from having expressed
and meant them, as if some great voice said

                                        be

and erased all other verbs.

Mother we call the beauty in
what cannot be possessed,
and *father*, where are you
but in the violence it takes
to create her?

In Apology

Some fears cannot be conveyed without metaphor—
          so please accept these

golden threads woven into a bundle, hundreds
of thousands of compact threads that compose
a single bale. Each holds tight its brilliance, initiates
yet succumbs in the end to the brilliance
of the whole. Body upon brilliant body. Bone sparked
against bone, a quiet fire over a field
          so flat and forever.

          *

Not even earth can describe our harvest, not even the sky
in all its burning can speak for ash.
               But there comes a time
abstractions must choose what shape to take.

For *justice*, please look down into my hands
as into a mirror. For *truth*, here's
a cord of kindling. For *you*, a midnight river of stars.
Impermanent knowledge brilliant disrepair fire—

                         I am sorry I am sorry I am

so sorry for describing *us* as bundled and aflame
and the beginning and end of light. *Light* is flat and forever
as a tree's shadow at sunset.

This Place of Scraps

Winter wastes nothing.
Even the fleshes petrified by frost find a home in the empty
belly of time.
Unearthed by sun to become myth someday, and I should be happy
to have my bones so repurposed and realized.

*

Even so, our house beneath the earth groans for more.
The inner workings fill with a predatory hunger.
We speak of what we have from what has been taken,
await completion like the offerings of empty-handed wise men.

*

And of firmament and soul.
Patterns reassemble earth into bridge. There is a crossing,
just there, where the monument has fallen.
Let's orchestrate language next time to resemble how it was, if it was.

*

The windfall of apples, of which there is no trace. Even the red
that was our blood has been licked clean and converted into energy.
Winter is hardly enough to believe in tomorrow.
Still I hang from the branches of a tree that might not be there.

*

And as if we weren't already born into death, we've written in the
snow a word that means *god*
and another that means *nothing* and another for *winter*.
Shuffled among them, already thawing,
I should be happy to be told: *in the beginning, as the end, there was
only this.*

A Dead Boy Distinguishes Proximal from Distal

Whispers of birds,   sometimes
a memory   vagued by its periphery.
Things defined by their nearness
to words   and how tight to center
we hold what was meant.
Think of grandfather's hands
steepled softly over his plate.
They say somber   simple things
like *sin*,
I cannot undo,   music.
I learned young the difference
between feeding and being   fed,
pushing and the pushed.
Think   of the unshaped birds
he did not intend to release in me,
that still are   in the margins
moving closer.   Somewhere
between what his hands meant to say
and what I heard,   the moment
our bodies passed each other into memory.

I Sit My Grandfather by the Mouth
of the Columbia River

Because he'd never seen either coast, I sit his ghost down
where my new river empties out. Where freshwater becomes salt.
Where I try to forget where we came from.

I tell him it's called an estuary. He cannot wash himself
from past landscapes.I tell him it's called purging.
He still decorates the sky with iron birds.

Waves continue to bash against us
like the maelstrom of wartime machines.
You are no longer what you were, I whisper
like a lullaby over an emptied cradle,

and you will always be alongside me,
where you've never been. His response
is a kind of silence different from midnight's calm,

different from water losing itself in water,
the distance between us reduced to unshared terrain.

He tells me that nothing can fully know its name.
I hold up his diary that christens each casualty.
He tells me absolution is an act of self-resistance.
I remember the cornfields as *so far from here,*

the flat, arid valley that drowned us
and for which we drew blood,
how full a silo feels when emptied of everything but our bodies.

Bone River (ii)

Bodies went
unburied that year, this year, last night as the elders formed a river
around our high-banked kitchen table, faces blackened by candle-
light, and moved their mouths in prayer.
I am uncertain what is made of earth and what assembles in the
mind from shovelfuls of earth. I wrote *go to the light*, but the bodies
went uneaten by the light in the earth. So I wrote *salve*. I believed in
gesture.
I hope the need for forgiveness forgives me.

All night my body went and came back into this
room with the candle.

Eulogy

Strange knowing you will never breathe this air.
Though the ashes I release,
unburdened by your name,
swirl out and circle back without purpose,

I would like to believe
the dead can also yearn
for wild trajectory,
be as liberated by a mountain at dawn.

I would like to believe we can share
this abandon,
that ash can remember.

Nearby, birds
are defining themselves by their song
and I can feel the river far below
cleansing these hands
that look too much like yours.
Even the distant motorboats echo
into proximity.

I am still no closer to knowing
how much of you is here.

I sit in this open cathedral
bequeathing what you've given me.
To this free
living air, the black
powder of your lungs.

To the mountain,
where your bones end
and rock begins.
To what is missing,
what remains.
What remains?
And must there be a name for it?

Mother's Day

The emptiness around us
forms a solid presence:
I can shave my face
with a memory,
wash my hands
in her eyes;
one morning every year
I'm allowed to plant color
back into dead flowers,
warmth back into
the cemetery bench.

Sanctuary

A star rests heavy on the roof.
A dozen dead birds roost in the gutters.
When it rains it's as if everything
were born iron, every structure built
to leak from the corners.

A disembodied swing set arcs
and punctures the sky. Through the hole
a familiar letter tumbles to the lawn. To be happy
all we can do is read about ourselves in the past.
Do you remember? and again
and again and the birds
descend dead to the window
we've never opened. And the star.

II.

I Go to the Ruined Place

—for Sam Roderick Roxas-Chua

Immigrant
I walk the town that raised me.

I study the estranged hues
of once-known trees—
   so many blacks, whites,
   a handful of birds,
   forgotten flight patterns.

I follow the street
that winds along the river
down to my quivering lower lip—
   shattered mirror in my blood,
   brick behind my back.

Windows
so like my eyes
stare back, foreign,
from the corner house
with broken lashes.

Distant,
I can hear a dead boy
still marking the walls
in crayon

inside.

Hemophilia

Grandfather's blunt
and calloused railroad hands
and his wife's silent
fingers pricked from planting
mustard seeds and
their daughter bleeding
from every line in her palm.
And from a hole in her belly. I
was new once. Entrenched
in myself. Knowing

I'd be the one to get away with it,
this time. Knowing all is forgiven,
remade once the blood dries.
With eternity behind us
we were not meant to be
this broken.

    Breaking,

now I wonder how often they said
my palms will pierce differently
under these same lamplit bed sheets making
dream birds from the same

    dreams.

Calligraphy

All these elegant black
forms / isolated universes
beholden to every other /
each twisted oak limb that haunts
night's grass and is part
of a body / the unfinished
chrysalis of river water becoming
sea / I cannot follow my
line's trail into meaning without
injury / to write you into the world
would imply continuity / and I'm not ready
to reconcile fatherhood with the hope
of a son / ink spills into the next / shadows
stand guard at the root of each object
and the light

Postpartum

He doesn't know the consonants of our waste.
He can't yet speak the vowels of ruin.
Perhaps it would be better if he never broke
from the frail bars of the cradle
into this vaguer cage.

I fear his sudden humanity.

So he won't dream too far from things
I tear north from every map,
then I tear off the center. I take
down the photographs, sew shut the curtains,
go about eyes closed so he cannot see himself
in my mirror.

His grandmother weaves a red flower through his black
spindly hair. I take away her hands.
And her tongue, all those crippled stories
of hope. Light and the shadows we must endure to feel
its warmth. I snuff out the candles.

But every day he screams himself out
of that infant darkness, and someone
keeps opening the windows.
My clenched and trembling
eyelids, as much a mirror.
I fear for when he learns his face
is not a place of refuge.

In the Kingdom of Moths

Why are there no more birds, he
asked me this morning from the center
of our dead lawn, his eyes
on the broken sky, stone and
shards of stars in his hand / *why
can't I hear their music anymore*

I tell him *nothing
exists that is not for you /
we must create
the forest to burn the forest*

as I watch his curious fingers widen
the holes in his coat / as early
winter enters / I don't know
if he's already stopped

feeling the cold / if he sees
the moths
as they eat away the fabric

A Dead Boy Martyrs His Mother

With two intersecting boards
and a skyful of nails.

With a backpack of black powder
and disassembled machinery.

With a sanctified blade
to behead or slip between
ribs like a love letter
returned to sender.

With white robe
stretched over a lake's calmness,
her hair fisted, submerged,
a kind of baptism.

With night's cold vigil— words,
more words, clasped hands
and the suggestion of candle.

With one holy book or another,
in this case the story she repeated
over his cradle as mantra
about a naked man bound
ceremoniously to rebirth.

He needs to know
if boulders move on their own
from the mouth of an empty cave,

how to distinguish love

       from grief.

Procession

A city's worth
of wooden christs.
Handcrafted sorrow.
Just for today
heavy as devotion.
Streets awash with controlled
self-flagellation.
(The secret is animal blood,
paintbrushes, and guilt.)
Eyes broken earthward. Eyes turned
toward the clouds in the earth.
The flower's remedy the same
as the flower's poison.
Set the paper bull aflame.
And run.
But not from the sparks
or heat or
each other—
the ash,
our footprints in the ash,
where the footprints lead us,
(*away* another word for
nearer) nearer.
As if our hearts
were not already in it.
My heart
is not yet in it.
This dazzling
confederacy of losses.

Every color red.
I can only be as broken
as (if *fear* is another word
for *love*)

love.

Pompeii

A winter olive grove sculptured like death-
distorted bodies. Pale light in the trees. An outline of lost
children in the paleness, though not in the light. Tears of stone

emerge from angels frozen to walls. Against them
my face stands translucent / my smallest gestures
multiply and mean.

/ apart from eternity nothing here isn't ash /

Beside me, a daughter imprisoned
in her mother's arms. For a moment
I am the boy whose limbs cannot / break
or move.

And there are dogs
forever fetal, almost unborn / all
around me / what I think
are men being converted
into music. I can play white
through their mouths / through the echo
of their screams / white through their teeth
forever snarled at the heavens.

A Room for Listening

I hold closest the places I've never been;

the silent history of *Grandfather*, which is only a word
for uninhabited house, alive in my cheekbones, hairline, dreams,
not even a whisper in the conch of my ears

made of hands and images

brother who died before knowing breath
or heartbreak, leaving us clay to mold him
into the tree of our choosing; how I was born
vibrant as the sun angled through his branches
from this same womb

an empty room remembers

suicide by forgetting, aunt clung to my elbow
—*Father?Brother?Son?*—perhaps there was a time
I could have been all of these things; it was not then
or now

how a piano once played here,

cousins who flew fifteen hundred miles in different directions
to escape a legacy of locks;
from that distance how he seems so much nearer
and forgiven

without keys

mother is lost within an intricate whiteness—
sheet, gown, bedside carnations, body
heavy as a late autumn snowflake; what sustains
is no longer the same blood that is in me, but
my veins can taste it

how we still know it as song

low. winter. sun.

Half-light through cold bodies
of clouds. A city loses itself around the edges.
From last night's rain upon the snow: fog.
The steeples and towers of glass vanish.
What's left of the sun teeters on low-hanging
neon, cracked pavement and puddles, hurts
my eyes when it finally breaks.
The white birds of morning go gray
from cutting restless paths
through an imprecise sky. There is no ledge
to call home anymore, no heads
to our greening statues, no heaven
for our raw hands. Heavy as warm
bodies of clouds, all things come
to roost temporarily on my skull.
I accept their poetry as part of living
so low, in the center of a city
with shattered windows.

Alight

The bird tells me how to read it.
From an air-filled perch the bird tells me
only our meanings are false.
Whether I claim nimbus cloud or empty sky,
whatever I name *dry* and try to possess
the rains will bully into being wet.

The bird tells me I am half wrong about this,
that I will always be exactly half wrong.

The bird tells me every gesture is worthy
of language, but not the other way around.
So I point at the bird and say *exile.*
I say *exile* and find nothing in my mouth.

There's a stone in my pocket and another in my hand. This,
I believe, is what they call "the best of both worlds."

But I am half wrong about this

and half wrong about the bird,
grown silent and stiff

over a landscape that died unburied
long before I had the chance to love
or desecrate it.

Bone River (iii)

At night, sometimes, I hear them
grind dreamlessly against cold sheets,
                longing

for something not yet named. Those
perfectly formed hands, so like mine,
alive with unrevealed obligations.

It is night sometimes
and from the cradle her eyes
appear as fire breaking over water.
Her body is beginning to remember itself—
what is it here I have left unbroken?

A Dead Boy During the Dry Season

There's only so much water
to divide between fresh and salt,
to wetten a dying boy's lips
and to wash him with after.

But our rituals demand this
comfort and cleansing.

Please
think of me as an ocean,
he said to his mother
as if in apology.
I think she prayed
over his body
and drained the home's well
in reply.

To keep the barren sky at bay, his brothers
danced the rain from each derelict cloud.
His father unburied six generations
and collected their tears in a wooden pail.
The house emptied its gutters. The house empty
of walls.

The narrative goes something like
death must wait for the draught to resolve.

Now his lips are soft as a muddy embankment. The earth waits hard
and dusty as skin.

Away from Stillness

You leave the womb
of our bed and outside
wait for the weather
to change again.
The blood that once
impregnated the sky
has whitened to snow,
and for six months
we have tried to return
from barren winter
to that raw place
of hope.
I wade deep
and naked
into your absent half
of the mattress
as you wait deep
inside night,
wreckage of the moon
falling into your hands.
Through a closed window
I hear you clearing off
our wounded road
so he can finally see
his tiny, unformed name
written in eulogy

beneath all this snow.

Echo Chamber

—for my mother

My back against the flat field.
All the arms I have ever known
constellate around me,
countable and temporary stars
that only shine when staring
into the darkness around them.

There is a reason I am here
waiting for the grass to consume me,
cradled by your hands your light

yet even this intimacy
is called *remoteness*.

*

No conversation between planets,
just a silent pull a silent push
which mean the same thing
when orbiting a body
that is not there.

*

And heaven
were it any different
than waiting in a field
for the absent

to return

and hell
were it any different;

there is a reason you are here
cradled by my hands my light—

the dead still have too much to lose.

A Dead Boy Learns Metaphor

The poetries of white blood cells
        help us make sense of the body.

The comfort of abstraction,
     of self-defining
          by our creations.

     Something clots.

I rename the white hospital walls *swans*.

Now they are feathered   and I

        can finally be their pure spring lake.

The wolves at my bedside say my heart is an ocean
so I construct a simple ark to fit two of each limb.

The sheets are a canvas of long-

            fallen leaves
so I rake my fingers over cotton and gather their falling.

The flowers they've left me will decay like a star.

When they burst into grief   I'm told   other planets will
still see me for years
       trailing off like
silence between unstable words.

Miscarriage

This body, I can
only pronounce its shadow.
The rest we have taken
as a necessary silence;
his name buried deep
in the organ's rusty refrain,
his legacy clasped between
two hundred steepled hands,
his flight away from us etched
into someone else's book,
his voice drowned out by the praise
that is just another wall
in a house, like any other,
erected on undesigned earth.

Fertility

Can I say that a child died inside us
when all we have conceived is a name
for what could be?

We've built a cradle of nails and wood
to house a body too busy dying
to rest, a trophy of grief
we polish in case of tomorrow.

Yet still he cannot see through
the eyes I tried to give him.

My mother has woven a shroud
to warm the son, blue for the sky
and gold for its promise, black
around the edges to resemble
the distances between them.

Our friends have their mantra
the world will wait for you
and we have our reply
spelled out in silence.

Forth and Back

In the book, we seek a certainty
shaped by hunger to appear as land.

The *was* of paradise,
    unforgiving floodwaters
        that eclipse our little vessel.

The *is* of our hands,
    of what in us still is
        an honest belief in direction.

If both raven and dove return
    empty words,
        let's next send in our stead

      silence,

      let's rename the solid,
      rename the firmament,

      rehearse the disaster
      of never knowing either,

as we cannot live
where we say *house*

or translate our bodies

away from their trembling.

III.

For My Mother, in Parting

Written across the lake's restless
surface, why does the sun
read as a sorrowful path
that relies so heavily
on where it has been
and where it is going,
on our past burnings and the terrible
ash of no-longer-being?

It is good to remember to forget these things.

It is good to forget the sun—
regret, triumph, shadow
and the steady swell of time.
Immense and insistent
our hearts cannot hold all

the light it took to get us here.

Here,

where the tulips we've planted fold
into hands and our hands fold back
into seed and seed cannot stop
folding and folding up into blossom.

Welcome it.

Mother,

let's welcome everything
we are not and
will never be
into our hands
and rub them together like
clouds, like clouds, like
impossible clouds that hold
all the light of this impossible sun
that will never stop

    folding.

Frontiers

There and not there,
your young body lost
in a flurry of wheat fields.
As memories dim
only their landscapes endure.

In the corner of your eye,
a prairie falcon still burns
through valley-bound clouds.
You cannot unremember
those nests made of mouths and
tiny screams from the bottlebrush,

      carried off.

There are mountains buttressing
other mountains, in the hazy distance
fires that clear the way for autumn.
But you are nowhere in it.

Your mother's prayers, there at the edges.
Your sisters' broken toys, intact again.

When you're reminded there was a river
thick with perch that bent
under your childhood
window and trailed off
at the horizon,

      you cry.

Then you tremble
with laughter
and I tremble
with you.

The sky so small
catching up to us.

Preparations Have Been Made

We've unknotted
her brow,
massaged
her muscles limp,
unclenched each white-
knuckled finger
then both fists
then the heart.

We've wrapped her broken
skull in muslin and
passed it to the children
as a lesson.
We've wrapped her dreams
of us in burlap
and drowned them in the lake.

So why does she still scream
across the distances between us?

We remembered to sew
her mouth tight
with piano wire
but the manual doesn't say
how to silence
our listening.

A Dead Boy Fishes with His Dead Grandfather

The fish have broken the line again, Grandpa,
and everything we've held runs silver through our hands,
and out. Across the never-ending surface: disruptions and
echoes, waves our crooked fingers cannot flatten.
Our lines travel without us. You and I and the lives we must end.

But not today.
Today we've lost the death that keeps us.

Today we reverse: you are my child and I will love you
for the childish stories I've heard.
About the dead you cannot erase,
muddied uniforms and flags marked by the smallest red suns.
About how Grandma combs the long-dried blood
from your thinning hair, with her thinning hand.
About how each kindness is a reason to remain unpardoned.

How memory writhes below skin and is its own decision:
devour or release.

I will decide to love the empty hook of your body,
like a warning, your hands —
where they've calloused and where they've healed.
Today I will pretend to understand

why you cry like a knife stroke when I throw you back.

House on Fire

The silhouette of animals
stacked skyward   face upon wooden face
on the shore of this
      now-unpronounceable river

can be called *origins*.

Language adjusts to sight,

and what the gull sees is not
     what the Haida saw, is not what I see
when holding   the earth
         flat
         by its history.

Meaning has always been   forfeit.

This applies as much to love
      as to the living
tree hollowed out to enunciate *love*
           as to the burning
beams that support my home,
stacked near-heaven like smoke,
and carved from the myth
of grandmother's white bones.

A Dead Boy Counts

Often I walk the wall dividing us.

Hollow stones   and   sun-blackened moss.

I count quietly the shoes I've worn through to get here,

each untied lace,   clipped wing,   broken bit of
soil.

Small things snug in my small eye,

without context   taking on   eternity.

I thought it was searching that defined destination.

Without destination   I have only   my small
footprints:

      a jar of baby teeth still lodged under my pillow.

      A certificate bearing only the numbers of me.

      A half-open window. A wall to keep you outside.

      The *where* of my body. The *how* of your remembering.

Teething

An unbroken wail across the long waking
hours, the body beginning
to know itself. Skin ruptures
to make room for enamel, which is to say
we are meant to be a harder structure.

But for me to promise *suffering*
is easier once you eat of it
would be like claiming the maple
outside her window learns to endure
its shadow, that birds in time enjoy the tension
between eating and being eaten
by something larger. If

      I can be trusted with truth

I would tell her how bittersweet things taste
once she's ripped them from the earth
and bitten down, which is how
I've come to know my father and how she
will come to know me.
The shadow of love thickens under a hesitant tree.
    Darling,

I'm not ready for your wailing to stop.

Say Bang

No longer can I build temporary structures.
As my son's castle washes gently back to sea
the walls I have molded from sand remain

hard into winter. I write *shame*
on both of our chests though the ocean
erases only one of these brands.

The weapon he boyishly fires
at gulls returns to driftwood the moment
he forgets our war.

I aim the same stick at his heart,
say *bang*, and his body
we buried last night under sea foam and moonlight.

Now when I try to wash my hands of themselves
the entire ocean turns red and without resolution
my body alone unbuilds into sand.

A Dead Boy Fashions the Grand Canyon from His Body

Snow melts

and the ensuing river begins to wear down the mountain

drop by infinitesimal drop—a process of hollowing.

    *

Nobody recognizes his own unbecoming,

so the slow green slope of us

       slopes slowly into blue.

    *

They say it takes full centuries to erode a body
       completely.

I'm not so sure. I was once a single misplaced word

that extinguished a family forever.

    *

Stone must be easier to revisit with hindsight

       to love more in its absence.

Stone must be easier to forgive.

*

One day we'll all have to travel a thousand miles and back

in a car too small for its family — over stone and sand —

just to stand awe-struck on the lip of some empty canyon

carved from a mountain by a dried out river.

The Cultural Narrative of Clouds

The sky is a girl abandoned naked by the river,
clouds swollen and purple
by light's unthinkable angle.
Too young to spell *moon*
or her mother's name.
Born ghosted. An offered fig
at the foot of the temple.
Think Mumbai in summer: barechested men,
bruised fruit in their hands.
Think how seeds ripen early
in the unlikeliest places.
Still there is love to be born
from unintended horizon
or shoveled dead into the waves,
weighed down to stars.

Penance

Those aren't mothers and fathers;
they are ships mooring us to the wild,
bottomless sea.
Those aren't the great
thinkers of yesterday
from which the story
of our times was built;
they are sarcophaguses.
The six-bladed star
and the sharply crescented moon
and the man hung from a piece of wood;
they are the one desert
we carry within us.

Those aren't pails of oasis water
we've hauled over sandy miles
despite ourselves, home
to wash our dying
daughter's body;
they are only prayers,
and we

aren't mothers and fathers
anymore.

Forbidden Travel

The lawn is the same
but has forgotten my toes,

my nakedness, a dog for the chain
still wound around our maple.

Bowed roof and black
creases of wall and a missing

word for *home* that once lightened
nightmared corners.

I have lost maturity's detachment.
I fear the distances I've traveled,

what has changed and could be gained
from return. And I want again

for all impossible things,
like the lessons of stars,

the immediacy of embrace,
the simplest words

embedded in gesture.
I want again for all impossible

unsullied things,
like a fistful of stars,

a fistful
of meaningful stars,

an impossible destination
to warm their bodies.

A reliable compass
made of broken arms.

Paper Cranes

They cling to the walls
of our daughter's room and all
around the house, poorly folded
from the unread morning news.
We like to believe
what we make will save us. Before
our weddings and our births and after
someone's left us and sometimes
for no other reason
than to give our hands the illusion
of control.

      Outside, we have
a stone dial that reads the sun by its shadow.
Outside, a stranger's story repeats itself further
from our ears.
The birds outside drink
from a dried out fountain.
While inside we like to believe

      we will be saved
by a rustle of paper
mimicking flight
and our daughter who cries
when she sets them free to sink

in the bathtub, all around her.

To Name Butterfly

Suffocated
in a bell jar,

dried into some
paper-thing
on a ledge
dusted by sun,

propped upon a fine
background,
poked at,

wings pinned back
to avoid death's
flight

and interrogated

by genus, species,
the Latin behind
our current tongue,

caked in the dream
of understanding
what we already know to be true:

otherness

is the name for forgetting
how to turn our heads and ask.

A Dead Boy Visits the Grotto

It's not god I fear   these roads will wind toward
but concave rock   hollowed to fit my fist.

In the center of me stands   one
gleaming statue, unmovable,
that always catches the light just right
or is caught   and held   by the sun
like crucifixed arms   like
the varied meanings behind a lake of candles   like prayer
if one could pray by burning.

I fear even history is a garden   of man-made stone.

Then there's the stream, always
an incision of fresh water
leading up to the foot
of the foot
of the promise.

I wash my own feet and remember grandmother's eyes
hollowed to fit belief.

Eventually the light wanes;   that is to say

I cannot stop my fist from smothering it.

Each road ends in stone;   that is to say

please.

Lullaby for the Damned

Go ahead and scream, little one,
while your voice still holds an echo.
Wail yourself violently
into a peaceful sleep
and dream
that this house we share has ears.

It is okay to thrash
your tiny arms and legs
and eyes and soul
impotently in the air.
It is okay.
I will thrash with you.
I have never stopped
thrashing
or wailing.
It is all that remains
from what we're given.

Now lay your weightlessness here on my chest
and listen to what must sound like my heart.
It has not been *a heart* or *mine* for many years.
But it can still beat in you.

Optimism

Our children do not listen anymore.

The clay has spun free
of the potter's wheel.

It will not harden.

What are we to do
with these broken,
idle hands?

Wisdom ricochets off
without penetrating.

But still we fire.

We are an optimistic
people.

Though the whole
of human history
corroborates our story

our children do not listen

and may finally

  save us.

Bone River (iv)

Calm and glassy eye of winter, river surface silenced.
Is it fair that not everything ends?

Dear breath, prepare for storm. Dear copse, devoid of wrens.

There are wild hinterlands just inside the door too. For example, I
am learning to brush my teeth with kindling,
scrub the enamel down to fire.

It's where I speak from nowadays.

Damn the slow sky bluing—mostly for us.
Damn the loose earth shoveled over the hard packed earth below.
Dear revenant, how much longer can I hide in you?

Dear wrens-

Denouement

Prayer flags heave like healthy lungs beneath a five colored sheet.
Wind is implied. Or breath. Healing. But definately movement.

All the weightless things around us convulse into terrible
ghosted forms, then return to their tenacious dangling.

The world ages at the rate we expect it to.
We are not so fortunate

as cricket legs at dawn. Here is the dawn:
caked translucent light, war painted heavens

steadily retreating, bewildered impulse
to enter the house and leave the house

without opening a door. Here is the door;
it's grown smaller than a child's body

and fits our burning. It fits her body.
I shine a flashlight up

to where hours ago we misidentified the North Star.
Temporary light. False light. We've lost as much

in going as in her being
gone. *Go,* I whisper, though she doesn't

seem to hear much anymore as the boydy hum
slows into earth. Breath weakens its search

for more of the same. On the porch between us stars
are implied. Or roots. Her shoes with just enough wind left

inside them.

About the Author

John Sibley Williams is the editor of two Northwest poetry anthologies and the author of nine collections. A five-time Pushcart nominee and winner of the Philip Booth Award, American Literary Review Poetry Contest, Nancy D. Hargrove Editors' Prize, and Vallum Award for Poetry, John serves as editor of *The Inflectionist Review* and works as a literary agent. Previous publishing credits include: *The Midwest Quarterly, december, Third Coast, Baltimore Review, Nimrod International Journal, Hotel Amerika, Rio Grande Review, Inkwell, Cider Press Review, Bryant Literary Review, RHINO,* and various anthologies. He lives in Portland, Oregon.

Apprentice House is the country's only campus-based, student-staffed book publishing company. Directed by professors and industry professionals, it is a nonprofit activity of the Communication Department at Loyola University Maryland.

Using state-of-the-art technology and an experiential learning model of education, Apprentice House publishes books in untraditional ways. This dual responsibility as publishers and educators creates an unprecedented collaborative environment among faculty and students, while teaching tomorrow's editors, designers, and marketers.

Outside of class, progress on book projects is carried forth by the AH Book Publishing Club, a co-curricular campus organization supported by Loyola University Maryland's Office of Student Activities.

Eclectic and provocative, Apprentice House titles intend to entertain as well as spark dialogue on a variety of topics. Financial contributions to sustain the press's work are welcomed. Contributions are tax deductible to the fullest extent allowed by the IRS.

To learn more about Apprentice House books or to obtain submission guidelines, please visit www.apprenticehouse.com.

Apprentice House
Communication Department
Loyola University Maryland
4501 N. Charles Street
Baltimore, MD 21210
Ph: 410-617-5265 • Fax: 410-617-2198
info@apprenticehouse.com • www.apprenticehouse.com

CPSIA information can be obtained
at www.ICGtesting.com
Printed in the USA
LVOW08s1353291216
519127LV00001B/71/P